Shoot The Pastor
A Practical Guide to Television Ministry

Donald New

Published by DreamSire Entertainment, a SummitWide Holdings, Inc. company, Johnson City, TN 37615

ISBN 978-0-615-25576-7

Cover Design: DreamSire Entertainment Copyrighted © 2008

Edited By Linda Germain

Dedication

I would like to dedicate this book to Krista Loury. She has been a great encouragement and my biggest supporter during the writing process. I would also like to thank all the people who have taught me through the years. The ones who have taken their time and unselfishly helped me grow in the knowledge of television and ministry.

Table of Contents

Foreword

Donald New has written an incredible book
concerning television ministry. In "Shoot the Pastor,"
he describes the role of television personnel and
their place in the ministry. He elevated the level of
television beyond the craft to the place of actual
ministry.

Donald New came to Calvary Church where I pastor.
He was not looking for position in the ministry; no, he
was seeking God's will in the choice of a home
church. Donald already had a job at a local television
network. His heart's desire was and still is to serve
God first and to be a blessing within his local church.

Donald served faithfully as a volunteer in any way
that he could help ministry. It wasn't long, however,
before everyone around him recognized his talents
and gifting in television and his leadership gifting to
mentor others to honor God in their callings.

As you read this book you will glean practical insight
from his years of experience as well as spiritual
principles for the development of this key area of
ministry. You will learn specifics, such as:

- How to start a television ministry: The Calling and The Commitment

- How to develop a Television Ministry: The People and the Production

- How to Improve a Television Ministry: The Cosmetics, The Cameras, The Sound and the Systems

- How to Lead a Television Ministry: Management, Manpower, Means, and Maintenance

With all the struggles and expense that television ministry can encounter, it just makes sense to prepare if God has called you to television ministry! This book will help you prepare to improve and succeed.

Dr. Richard L. Hilton
Senior Pastor Calvary Church,
Bishop-Calvary Alliance of Church and
Ministries

Introduction

You should always aspire to grow in knowledge and to move forward with your ministry. That includes television. I will cover some things in detail, but this book by no means is expected to be the end of all information you will need to be effective in this medium. There is a wide variety of textbooks and training manuals available that I believe can help you become even more successful. While those textbooks focus solely on the production side of television, this book incorporates production elements in tandem with our obligation as Christians.

That same day Jesus went out of the house and sat by the lake. Such large crowds gathered around him that he got into a boat and sat in it, while all the people stood on the shore. Then he told them many things in parables, saying: "A farmer went out to sow his seed. As he was scattering the seed, some fell along the path, and the birds came and ate it up. Some fell on rocky places, where it did not have much soil. It sprang up quickly, because the soil was shallow. But when the sun came up, the plants were scorched, and they withered because they had no root. Other seed fell among thorns, which grew up and choked the plants. Still other seed fell on good soil, where

it produced a crop—a hundred, sixty or thirty
times what was sown. He who has ears, let him
hear.   -Matthew 13:1-9 (NIV)

I am referencing the scripture in Matthew because we are talking about television *ministry.* This scripture will help clarify the importance of the following three concepts you need to grasp when you are part of a television ministry:

1. There are some standard practices in television production that, if followed, will help you achieve excellence in your television ministry and create a quality program for broadcasting. More often than not, the Christian broadcasters I see do not aspire to excellence. In Matthew 13, the Word talks about that **seed** which had no root because the soil was shallow and because of that it died away. As Christian broadcasters, when we allow ourselves to do things without quality, or without excellence, it is just like that shallow soil. If a program is done poorly, people simply will not watch, and that gives the seed of God's Word no chance to take root.

2. The competition we have is not the other Christian programs on television. In reality, the competition is every program on television that distracts and pulls people away from the Christ message and a life of

Godliness. We need to produce television programs that will deliver the **powerful message of Christ** in a more effective way than that programming on television which is like the thorns in Matthew 13: 7. We do not want to choke the seed and cause it to die.

3. There is a right way to create television programming. When the decision is made to start in television, it is just as important to make the decision to do it in the most excellent manner possible. Now, I must tell you right up front, if you do it the right way, it is going to take money. I know that subject is somewhat taboo when talking to a lot of Christians, but the simple fact is, **television is expensive** if you do it right and with professionalism. So, if you are not willing to pay the price, then my recommendation is to just not do it.

As I said before, and will keep reiterating, when we do it **right** it becomes like that good soil and will produce a harvest. As you read this book, my hopes are that it will give you a clear understanding of why this is important, but more than that, an understanding of how to accomplish it.

The Bible tells us that God's people are destroyed for lack of knowledge. That is why this little book is so important. It will give you the knowledge necessary to start and sustain a successful television ministry; plus, it will help people who are not involved in the television ministry to understand its importance.

Pastors and leaders, you will benefit by having a clearer understanding of:

1. What it actually takes to produce a television program or product.
2. How important you are to the program's success.
3. The demand television will create for you as a pastor or leader.

Television personnel and volunteers:

1. You will realize your place in the ministry.
2. It will help you deal with the simple fact: it *is* a ministry and there is something greater involved than just producing a television program.
3. And, it will help others to comprehend your role in the ministry.

Lay people:

1. You will be able to see television as something more than just a program.

2. You will realize the importance of television and how it can benefit a church willing to do it right.
3. And, it will help you recognize the need for your support.

Again, I want to say this book is **not** intended to be a complete training manual or textbook for production. Its intent is to enlighten you on things you may not understand in television and how it can be an effective ministry tool. I would hope it would answer some of the questions you might have prior to starting a television ministry and help you make your television ministry more efficient -- if you already have one.

Take One:
Beginning A Television Ministry

As you begin to read, it may seem as though this first chapter is directed mostly toward pastors, leaders, or persons making the decision to begin a television ministry. These decisions are directly related to everyone involved in the ministry, not just the leadership. So, I implore you to read on.

Determine Your Calling

As a consultant to ministries who are making the decision to begin television production, the first thing I tell them is *to make sure God is calling you* to start a television ministry. This decision has to be first and foremost. I want you to know: Having an **opportunity does not always equal a calling**.

In *Ephesians 4:11-13 the word says*, **"It was he who gave some to be apostles, some to be prophets, some to be evangelists, and some to be pastors and teachers, to prepare God's people for works of service, so that the body of Christ may be built up until we all reach unity in the faith and in the knowledge of the Son of God and become mature,** *attaining to the whole measure of the fullness of Christ."(NIV)* **And in** *Psalm 37:23, "The steps of a good man are ordered by the LORD: and he delighteth in his way."(KJV)*

Simply said, it is **God who directs.** He is the one who calls you to ministry. He is the one who guides your steps. Therefore, it is important to seek Him and make sure that it is His desire for you to begin in television. A lot of times we all fall into the trap of trying to keep up with others. We often judge our success in life, occupation, and other areas by what we see in other people. Believe me, television is not an endeavor you want to get involved in to try and keep up with others. It is foolish to get involved in a broadcast television ministry if God is not leading the way.

When you have made the decision to go for it and begin producing a television program, you need to understand it should be as much of a priority as any other ministry in which you are involved. In a number of the ministries with whom I have worked when it came time to create a shooting schedule there always seemed to be something standing in the way. While shooting, the minister would often make comments about the length of time it was taking. Frequently they would schedule meetings or other engagements, not realizing this prevented the production crew from having enough time for to get everything taped. This casual and unprofessional approach to television creates multiple issues, which also leads to the necessity for more days of taping; again cutting into everyone's schedule.

Just like being the pastor of a church or the leader of a ministry, you must realize, when you host a television program, whether preaching from the pulpit or whatever style of program you decide to produce, *you become the face of the broadcast*. When a person asks me where I attend church and I answer them, often times, especially if they are unfamiliar with the church, the next question they ask is who the pastor is. Why is this? Well, it is because the pastor represents the church as its leader, just as a CEO is often the face of a company. **That is why you must make your television ministry a priority.** (When I say *priority*, please understand, I mean setting an importance to it equal to your other ministries. I understand the *ultimate priority* is the message).

The other issue you tend to face by not giving your involvement with television enough priority is *animosity with the production staff*. To the people involved in the production of your program, the importance they place on it is directly related to the importance *you* place on it. If you are reading this book as a person involved in the production of a ministry program, you need to realize this and try to keep yourself from feeling enmity toward the ministry, ministers or anyone in leadership because of a perceived lack of interest in the television ministry on their part. As a leader, you need to realize the success of your television ministry is directly related to your attitude and interest in it.

Finally, you need to strive for **excellence**. I will hit on this a number of times, but it is important to have as high a quality production as you possibly can. Never forget that people are accustomed to watching high quality programs and when you create something sub par it is often discounted as something not worth watching. ***The greatest message will never change anyone if it is never heard.***

I fully understand budgets and finances. At times, you need to start somewhere and it may not be possible to buy top of the line equipment, but you should not allow budgets and financial constraints to affect or limit your calling and vision. The issue is similar to other things in Christianity -- it is a matter of your *heart* and *mindset*. Even if you have a small beginning, have a *larger* vision!

A Vision for Television

We have all heard messages on the subject of vision, and most of them include *Proverbs 19:18,* ***"Where there is no vision, the people perish: but he that*** *keepeth the law, happy is he." (KJV)* In television this is a very essential truth. It takes a vision and lots of creativity to produce a quality television program that is interesting. But remember, the driving force that will keep people on track is the vision laid out by the leader; the "visionary" who God has placed as the head of the television ministry.

There are several areas to consider in the overall vision for the ministry. This includes what direction you plan to take your program, the reach or scope of the program and the organization of your media ministry or department. You need to have a clear-cut vision that can be communicated to the people to whom you entrust the ministry, the people you expect to support the endeavor of television, and for those unfamiliar to the ministry. In the Message Bible, *Habakkuk 2:2 says,* *"Write this. Write what you see. Write it out in big block letters so that it can be read on the run. This vision-message is a witness pointing to what's coming. It aches for the coming—it can hardly wait! And it doesn't lie. If it seems slow in coming, wait. It's on its way. It will come right on time."*

1. I cannot stress enough how important it is to make the vision plain. If it is stated succinctly and without compromise, questions about the television ministry can be easily answered by anyone involved.

2. You must develop a clear vision for the content of your broadcast. Are you just going to tape services and broadcast them? Are you going to run special advertisements for church events? Are you going to sell products? Are you going to let others be on the program? All of these are questions that should be answered up front.

3. You must also have a vision for the people and their role in your television program. If you are a pastor and want to broadcast your sermons, are you going to include shots of others? If so, you should let them know. With so many churches broadcasting these days, it is a little easier for people to understand. Over time, your congregation and auxiliary folks will get used to the television cameras.

4. Informing the people of what type of financial obligations it may take is very important, because there is a little part in all of us who want to know where our offerings are going, which is not necessarily right, but it *is* reality.

5. Communicate! Make sure that if your vision includes others that it is clear and understood by those who will be involved directly, or even indirectly. If you do not have a church and want to start a program, you need to decide who will be on the program, if anyone, and begin to prepare these people. Some of the

ministries and productions in which I have been involved ran into small glitches with the issue of people who had no desire to be on television. Just because we have a great idea for something that involves someone else does not mean they agree with that one-sided vision. If you plan to have someone on your program as a guest, make sure to verify they really *want* to be a guest and if there are any limitations that may affect the program or production.

6. Finally, have a vision for the future! The most detrimental part of Christian broadcasting is ministries who are content with small beginnings. I am not saying we should despise small beginnings, but we need to get hold of a vision for bigger things. A great example: **The Israelites**.

We all know the story. God delivered them from slavery and bondage but, sadly, the majority of them could not see the vision for anything greater. When they saw the work involved they feared what would happen. They never received what God had for them, simply because they lacked vision for the future. The Israelites wanted to look backward at what they **had** rather than looking forward and seeing the possibilities with God!

Caleb and Joshua had a vision for greater things. They saw the possibilities God had for them and were willing to do whatever it took. They too started in slavery, but because of a *different outlook*, their lives had a *different outcome*. That is the same spirit you should have. No matter what the price financially, physically, mentally or spiritually, if God called you to do it -- **then do it!** When the going gets tough, as it is often prone to do in any project, **do not give up** and abandon what God has called you to do.

Important Budget Considerations

There are a number of areas you need to consider with regards to finances as you begin a television ministry. Believe me, you should expect the unexpected!

The church where I first worked as I began my career in television had to invest in several things you might not expect. They had to add new air-conditioning units because the heat created by new television lights completely overpowered the existing air-conditioning. This was not included in the initial planning of the television ministry and delayed the starting date. So, make sure to look at every detail and expect some things to surprise you.

Another required investment was adding more

electrical power. The building was originally erected to be a church, with no thought to television. When additional air-conditioning units, and powerful television lights were added, the amount of power coming into the facility was deficient. These unforeseen problems and costs were incurred prior to ever taping one television program.

Without question, there are some financial considerations everyone can expect to incur starting a broadcast.

1. Typically, you must first look at the possibility of needing a staff. I have seen many different ways in which churches have approached this, but normally you need to budget for some type of payment to personnel. It is up to you to decide what personnel you will have and if they will be paid or volunteer. I will discuss different approaches to this later in the book.

2. Also, you will need to purchase equipment, lighting, tape stock, and other supplies used for the simple operation of your television ministry. Depending on your choices, the costs here can vary dramatically. It would be impossible for me to give an estimate on what you will spend, but understand, the better product you start with the better product you will finish with.

3. You will need to decide on an outlet for your program. Consider the financial investment you will need to make to purchase airtime. Airtime, like equipment prices, varies with each station or network you choose to broadcast with. Larger stations and networks, as you would expect, tend to cost more. Also, different times of the day will have varied and multiple costs. All of this is typically based on the number of potential viewers. (Remember: The more people you can reach, the more it will cost).

[There are times when a station or network will give you "free" airtime but *be careful*. Often times there are strings attached].

There are multiple other considerations apart from the ones I have already mentioned. That is why my recommendation is **to seek consultation** when looking into your possibilities with networks and stations.

Consultation

I recommend you seek good counsel before you make the decision to begin a television ministry. It is not *just* a recommendation, but the word of God illustrates the importance of good counsel. *Proverbs 1:5 the word tells us,* **"A wise man will hear and increase learning, and a man of understanding will attain wise counsel."**(KJV)

It is simple -- really. When you have an issue with your cars you call a mechanic. When you have a problem with your electricity you call either the power company or an electrician. So, when you are starting to venture into television, is it not logical that you would call someone trained and experienced in television?

Please consider this a serious warning: Be careful listening to advice of people whose only credentials are their employment in the television industry, whether it is a television station, another ministry or any other media position.

When I said to seek good counsel, I meant **good** counsel. You cannot assume, just because someone works for another television ministry, or a television station or because they have the title consultant hanging on their office that they know what they are talking about. I worked for one television station where, due to budget constraints, many of their employees had little or no experience in television. Some of them were enrolled in school or had just graduated, but had very little real world knowledge. Many times I heard them giving misguided advice to

11

ministries with programs broadcasting on the station.

Let me say this in defense of the employees of that station, I know in my life, I had to grow and learn television. More often than not, it was the hard way! So, I am not criticizing them, I am simply saying, there are some who have no experience that would be of little benefit to you starting a new television ministry.

Also, beware of the "good Christian brother." I have seen a number of ministries who have ventured down the wrong path based on the recommendation of someone involved in their ministry that they thought was a reliable source of information. Needless to say, though their recommendations may have been in good faith, the recommendations were not the best possible direction for the ministry.

I am not saying that you cannot trust anyone, but it will cost you if you choose to listen to the wrong voice. Experience is one thing you should look for in a consultant. You need to find persons who are respected by their associates and **make sure you get recommendations**. Also, depending on what type of consultation they are giving you, try to look at some of their work.

When I had my first opportunity to work in television, it

was at a church in Texas. I took over for a couple of people who came from a highly successful television ministry with a wonderful broadcast. Technically, the ministry they came from probably had the best broadcast in Christian television at the time. But, the two people hired by the church actually had very little experience in production. Honestly, the only thing they knew were other people who could produce, edit and distribute the churches program; but the church was expecting them to do the job. There came a point when the church leadership figured out these two employees would hire others to do the work expected of them. To make a long story short, when they left the ministry and I took it over, the church was in the hole. A conservative estimate would be over $100,000 in the hole! The reason was not the cost of television, which is expensive, but it was *hiring the wrong people* to do the job. So, when you look to hire consultants, or anyone else in you television ministry, be careful to understand their background and their actual knowledge and abilities.

Television Terminology

This is a very minor point, but it is important that you learn a little bit of television **terminology.**

When I first started in television, I attended a National Broadcasters Convention. While there, I participated in a manufacturers mock game show. It was not for broadcast but rather just to attract people's attention to their company booth. During the game, we were asked what abbreviation S.M.P.T.E. represented. I was introduced as the producer of a nationally broadcast television program and yet, I sat there with no answer. When the time ran out and the host gave the answer, there was an almost unanimous accusatory response from the audience, "And you said you were a television producer!" Needless to say I was a little embarrassed.

So, there are a couple of reasons why I say you need to learn some of the terminology. One is for the simple fact that you will be taken more seriously by other television professionals. Also, you run a lower risk of being taken advantage of by someone who just is not reputable.

You are wondering what is S.M.P.T.E.? It is the abbreviation for Society of Motion Picture and Television Engineers. Simple!

Take Two:
Developing A Television Ministry

I have discussed the initial steps you should consider as you begin your television ministry. In this chapter, I will get a bit more detailed and talk about the actual development of a television ministry.

Standard of Excellence

The first thing you need to look at is setting a standard of excellence. I know I have touched on this already, but as Christians, it is of utmost importance to have a standard of excellence. Jesus was a perfect example of what we should aspire to in life; and we should have the same desire to be excellent in all that we do, not just television.

These standards apply to every aspect of the ministry. I will discuss several areas of development and the standards set for deciding on your purchases, the operation of the ministry, and the organization. As you develop all areas, you should look at the standards you would like to achieve and let them guide you.

Personnel

Of course, the most logical thing to do first is to make the decision on personnel. This is important because, depending on who is chosen to maintain the day-to-day operations of the ministry, your personnel may need to be involved in some of the decisions to be made during television development.

My first recommendation here is, no matter how you decide to organize the ministry, to have someone you know to be part of the personnel. In *1 Thessalonians 5:12-13 the word says, **"And we beseech you, brethren, to know them which labour among you, and are over you in the Lord, and admonish you; And to esteem them very highly in love for their work's sake. And be at peace among yourselves."(KJV)**

I know the context of this scripture is to know the ones who are over you in the Lord, but I believe it illustrates to us, as leaders, that we should also be careful to know who is working *in* the ministry. Therefore, it is important to find someone who is faithful and loyal to the ministry and who can watch out for things that may not be right. This is especially important if you have outside personnel coming in to work as part of the team. This person does not necessarily need to know television, but needs to have the ability to discern when things are not being held to the **standard of excellence** you have set and to the standards set forward by the word of God. Often times, this person can fill the role as a department head or manager. If you do not like those terms, a title of *Minister of Media* might be considered.

I want to give you an idea here of what you may be looking at when you are making a decision on your staff. I will discuss each position with more detail in the next chapter as I talk about finding the right personnel. Understand though, with a television ministry in a church, you may not need the same type of employees as that of a Christian television station. But, as your television ministries grow, you may need different recruits from time to time. If you are starting a television station or developing a ministry strictly for television, it is more than likely you will need more personnel than a church would need.

Some of the positions you may need to fill include director, producer, editor, audio technician, camera operators, video engineer, and lighting director. There are a number of different ways to fill these positions through volunteers or freelance workers, or a combination of both. Again, I will discuss these decisions and positions in more depth in the next chapter.

Organization

The second thing you should do is set up the structure under which you will operate. This can be something that goes through a progression, but there are some basic things you need to think about.

Of course, the authority structure of personnel will, by and large, be the initial starting point. Again, what I recommend is to make sure to have someone you know to be the leader, or **the one who oversees the ministry**. Whatever title you choose to give this person is irrelevant, but it would be good if the person could fill an active role versus a passive role in the ministry. Having television experience would be a plus.

After that, I believe the most important position you could have on staff would be an **editor**. Believe me, every position is important, but a good editor can save you many headaches and sleepless nights. No matter what you do with your program or how you structure your staff, the broadcast will always pass through the hands of an editor. Not only that, an editor can help everyone become better by helping them understand the needs of creating the program. This is especially important if you have an inexperienced staff or volunteers handling the majority of your production.

In the beginning you may not see the need, but over time you will face a huge problem if you do not work out a system to **organize your tapes**. When I first started working in television at a church in Texas, we got to a point, after a couple years of production, where we had so many tapes it was difficult to find the ones we needed. Due to the amount of tapes and the issues we had finding the ones we needed, we had to create a library system for organizing the tapes which took a two or three month period. Had we done it in the beginning, it never would have become as big an issue. It is kind of like running out of gas. When you leave your house and the fuel gauge is low, if you wait too long you will be walking. So, the earlier you fill up, the easier it will be on you. It is the same way with the tapes. The earlier you organize them, the easier it will be.

[A little side note to this, when I discontinued working there, the lady who took over the department took all the tapes off the shelves and rearranged them for the sake of creating more room. Then for years, and I am not exaggerating here, but *for years* I would receive calls from the personnel working in that television department asking me if I knew where tapes were. So, do not underestimate the need for organization].

Television requires a number of **schedules.** If you will develop these from the start it will spare many headaches. Of course, you will need a schedule for **personnel**, whether they are paid staff, contractors or volunteers. It is especially important if you use volunteers to maintain a schedule of when volunteers are expected to be involved for production. I have seen a number of ministries who scramble before service to find volunteers to operate a camera because they have not developed a schedule. It seems like a simple thing, but it can really hinder you if you do not have one.

Also, a **production schedule** needs to be started. This will let everyone know when things will be taped, edited and finished. The importance of this will become more evident as you begin to work on your production. When you have to scramble around schedules of pastors, or potential guests or volunteers, you will quickly understand its importance.

Finally, a **shipping schedule** is typically necessary. Most stations or networks require a program to be in their possession a couple of weeks in advance of its actual air date. Therefore, you need to understand the importance of finishing things on time and have a schedule of dates for sending programs to the different stations and networks on which you choose to broadcast. Knowing these programs need to be delivered a couple of weeks in advance, you should always have some kind of buffer built into your production. I would recommend at least four to eight weeks depending on the level of post-production you are doing. Sometimes your program may require an even larger buffer period.

If you are starting a television station as your ministry, let me recommend that you develop a policy of receiving programs at least two weeks in advance. If you do not, you will have no time to check the programs for quality and to make sure they can be broadcast. Hopefully, that will cut down on tapes arriving sometimes *minutes* before they are scheduled to air.

Equipment

We will get into more depth when it comes to equipment later in the book, but just as I did with personnel, I would like to give you some things to think about as you develop your ministry.

Equipment purchases will directly reflect the quality of broadcast you anticipate. In this day and age, consumer cameras look really good, but they are not intended for use as broadcast cameras. There is a reason they sell these cameras for consumer use.

Sure, it is possible to go out and spend a few hundred dollars and set up a camera to record your program.

And, if you can find a station or network willing to broadcast a program of this quality, it is possible to broadcast it. My question to you would be, **"Is this how you want to represent your Lord and Savior? Do you want to portray Christianity in that light?"** Please understand, I am not trying to condemn you if that is how you started, or if you are currently doing this, but I just want you, as a Christian, to understand we are contending against the likes of MTV, VH1 and other networks for the attention of our youth and there are multiple networks when it comes to children and adults. So, when we do something of less quality, it is really detrimental to our cause.

Earlier in the book I touched on some of this. So, I hope you understand where I am coming from when I say we need to have as **high quality** as possible. I understand small beginnings, but do not allow small beginnings to persist indefinitely. Have a vision for more! When making the decision to purchase equipment let your vision and standards of excellence guide you.

Some of the equipment you will need to invest in includes cameras, lighting, editing and audio gear, control room or acquisition equipment and depending on what type of program you are developing, you might need to buy or build set pieces. There may be more equipment you need, but this will give you an idea of where to start.

Consistency

The final thing I would like to discuss in this chapter is the importance of keeping your message consistent. I have seen a number of ministers who tried to preach one thing in their pulpit, but when it came to television they thought they needed to change their message. I do not know if they thought they needed to be like others on television or if they felt the message would not work or have the same impact, but you need to understand it is very important that you **preach the same message**. If it will work in church, it will work on television. If it will work on the mission field, it will work on television. The Gospel will be effective no matter where it is preached.

Take Three:
Finding the Right Personnel

Freelance versus Volunteers

When you begin to make the decision between using freelance personnel or volunteers understand there are definite advantages and disadvantages with either choice.

It is important that you weigh every possible scenario along with your overall vision for your television ministry before you make the decision. Being around ministry, I understand the desire to totally use volunteers, but television is a different kind of ministry. While it is technical, it is also creative. Many times a technically inclined person is not the perfect fit because of a lack of creativity, but then again a creative person may lack the technical skills needed. Therefore, it is important to make a wise decision about your personnel, including, but not limited to the decision between freelance personnel and volunteers.

Definitely, the biggest advantage you will have with freelance personnel is experience. Typically, a freelance worker has worked in production for an extended period of time and is familiar with the overall production workflow. Experience is the reason for their ability to work as a freelance person. Just like deciding on consultants, **be careful** to find the right freelance personnel. Typically, freelance personnel would have recommendations along with something which displays their past work, such as a resume tape.

The main disadvantage you face hiring freelance personnel would be cost. Because of the experience they have, they often have plenty of clients, and that enables them to charge more than others might expect for their services. With a little bit of research, you should be able to find out what the standard rates would be in the area you are located. Of course, the more experience a person has, the more you may be expected to pay.

With all that said, you should be aware that you will generally get a **better product** in less time **with freelance personnel** than you will with volunteers. So, if quality is your main concern you might really consider using freelance personnel, but if budget is your main consideration, you might debate on the use of volunteers.

With volunteers, the main advantage is twofold. A volunteer from the church will typically be more loyal to your television ministry because of the *second* advantage you gain from volunteers; hopefully, they have the same heart as the leadership. With the understanding that volunteers will often have a lack of experience, you must have a willingness to work with that. Having someone with the heart of the ministry could be crucial. It may often save the ministry money, but also it could save the ministry from embarrassing situations that could arise by having someone working in the ministry who really does not care about the ministry or the message being sent forth.

I hope you realize, there are freelance workers who may have the same heart as your ministry, but at times it may seem impossible to find them.

Obviously, the principal **disadvantage with volunteers** is their lack of experience and the learning curve they face in television production. As I mentioned earlier, television is both technical and creative and it is important to have people who can work in that type of environment. I have worked with volunteers for years in ministries, both church and non-church. I have seen people who seemed to be perfect television volunteer candidates because of their technical ability, but they were just unable to function. On the flip side, some creative people feel constrained by some of the technical aspects. So, when deciding on volunteers you need to realize television is similar to a nursery ministry. Not everyone is suited for the environment and *just because* *someone is willing* does not mean they are usable.

Paid Staff

As you begin your television ministry, for it to ultimately be successful, you will probably have some form of paid staff. My recommendation with regards to paid staff is keep it as small as possible, but make sure you have enough people to complete the necessary work without an unnecessary burden upon one individual. Most ministries who develop a television broadcast, or a media ministry "on the side," seem to hire one person. That person is often overworked and underpaid. I think this is due to the nature of volunteerism.

Churches and ministries are too accustomed to having the majority of their work done by volunteers. I feel this often leads to an expectation of employees to volunteer their labor. By this I mean, they will underpay and overwork their employees. This is not just in the area of television but also often in every position of employment.

I know the ministries are dependant upon offerings for the majority of all income. I believe it is important to volunteer to do things in the church, but in this case,

27

we are talking about the livelihood of a person. We, as Christians, expect secular businesses to pay people well and want the people in churches and the people who are serving God to be successful. But when it comes time for a ministry employee to be paid, often ministries will not step up to the plate.

Let me tell you, we preach faith, we preach about living by faith and all the while we have more faith in the guy smoking the cigar sitting behind his desk in a secular job then we do in **our God**. We believe more in the ability of that man to pay people than the ability of our God to provide the funds to pay ministry employees fare wages for their gift and service to the ministry. (It is a ministry. It belongs to God!)

I also want to mention, as an employee you should have a **heart to serve**. You should be willing to do more for God than any employer no matter how much that employer pays you. Also, you should understand at times you may be required to do more than is expected, but know that God is watching and that He wants to know if you are going to be **faithful in the little things** so that He can bless you with much more. This may be a dirty word in ministries, but my daddy use to tell us all the time to have a little **pride** in our work. We should allow our work to reflect the excellence of God through the excellence of our labor!

[I diverted off the topic a bit, but I truly believe God is watching each of us to see how we treat others in our business practices. With that said, as an employer, in ministry or not, His blessings will be in the same measure at which you bless your employees].

When I first started my career in television, I had the opportunity to spend a day with the production crew at Lakewood Church in Houston, Texas. At the time, for a ministry production department producing a nationally broadcast program in multiple translations and multiple versions for television networks and stations, if my recollection is right, they had no more than seven employees on staff. The point I want to get across is to **limit your staff** to only what is necessary and pay them for the labor of their hands and for the talents God blessed them with for service to His kingdom.

[In a side note, Lakewood did have some freelance workers who would help on days they taped their programs. They truly minimized their staff and utilized the people's talents].

There is one great advantage to having paid staff: **COMMITMENT.** With volunteers, sometimes there are limits to the extent of their personal investment, but when people are getting paid to do a job, their level of commitment goes up for some reason. Through the years of working with volunteer staffs and paid staffs I have found the turn over is much higher with volunteers. Therefore, you can spend less time in training and other orientation type tasks and more time on getting the work done with paid staff.

Finally, you really need to make sure, if you decided to have a paid staff, that the people you hire **have the same heart** as that of the ministry. I have discussed this earlier and I am sure I will discuss it again, but it is crucial to make sure your message is the same message your staff would preach. This is especially true with television, because many times these people are making the decision as to what is and is not broadcast on your television program. With that said, you need to understand that your nights will be spent much more peacefully if you do not have to focus your attention on every detail of your television ministry. If you have to do that, you might as well do the work yourself.

If you are on staff with a ministry, or will soon be hired to work for one, you need to realize the importance of this as well. You are the reflection of the ministry and your work in production is a representation of the ministry, but more important it is representative of **your God**. Therefore, you should set your goal to be the best representative you can. If you know there are major differences in what you believe and your potential ministry employer, or current ministry employer, you might look for somewhere else to work. I say this because you will never be happy, the product you produce will never be the best, and it will ultimately end up in a *not so good* situation. Make it a matter of prayer and know that God has a place for everyone and He will take care of His children.

Department Head/Media Minister/Production Manager

I would highly recommend, if you decide not to go with a paid staff and want to utilize volunteers or freelance workers, that you **at least create one position.** That would be a department head, media minister, manager or whatever other title you want to give the position. This person would become the buffer between the ministry leadership and the people and items involved in the media or television ministry. Otherwise, if you are a pastor or leader in a ministry, you will become the "go to" person and it will lead to multiple distractions and consume more of your time. Decision-making could be delegated to a trusted department head.

For some reason, it is easy to see the need for people in other areas such as youth, nursery, or children's ministry, but when it comes to television we overlook that simple fact. Let me tell you this though, your television ministry, if it is broadcast on a television station or network, is a direct link to people outside of your church. It will speak to more of the general public than nearly all of your other ministries. It will be a direct reflection of what your ministry is all about. So do not overlook its importance! Make sure to do what it takes to make it successful.

The basic duties of a television department head would be equal to those of a manager in any business. He or she would be responsible for managing the staff, whether volunteer or paid, and maintaining the scheduling for all your production needs. They would oversee the entire production of your program along with the distribution. Of course, they would also report to the church leadership on things pertaining to the television ministry.

Your department head could very well be a voluntary position, if you can find the right person to volunteer. But, more often than not, this position would require a person to be paid. I mentioned earlier in the book, the most important paid position you could look for would be that of **an editor,** and I still believe that. Therefore, if you could find a person who could edit and maintain the duties of a department head, that person would be invaluable to your television ministry!

Take Four:
Importance of Proper Lighting

As I begin to discuss the importance of lighting, I want to start by re-stating this fact: **Television done right is expensive**. It is not for the faint of heart and if you are not careful you will give into the temptation to try and do it "cheap." We serve a God that never did anything cheap for us. God was willing to give the most priceless gift, in His son, so that we might be saved, so please do not give into the temptation of being cheap. If God called you to create a television ministry, He will provide.

In *Luke 5:1-11 the Bible says*, ***"One day as Jesus was standing by the Lake of Gennesaret, with the people crowding around him and listening to the word of God, he saw at the water's edge two boats, left there by the fishermen, who were washing their nets. He got into one of the boats, the one belonging to Simon, and asked him to put out a little from shore. Then he sat down and taught the people from the boat. When he had finished speaking, he said to Simon, "Put out into deep water, and let down the nets for a catch." Simon answered, "Master, we've worked hard all night and haven't caught anything. But because you say so, I will let down the nets." When they had done so, they caught such a large number of fish that*** *their nets began to break. So they signaled their partners in the other boat to come and help them, and they came and filled both boats so full that they began to sink. When Simon Peter saw this, he fell at Jesus' knees and said, "Go away from me, Lord; I am a sinful man!" For he and all his companions were astonished at the catch of fish they had taken, and so were James and John, the sons of Zebedee, Simon's partners. Then Jesus said to Simon, "Don't be afraid; from now on you will catch men." So they pulled their boats up on shore, left everything and followed him."* (NIV)

Right here the Bible gives us a clear illustration of a simple fact; when God asks us to do something, He has provision already in store. I understand, at times you must improvise, but you should not maintain a vision of improvising. You should maintain a vision of provision from a great God.

There are people out there who would say, "It is not about the television program but it is about the message." Some would say, "We should not have to window dress the Gospel message." Or even, "All that matters is if it has the Spirit of God, the anointing." But, let me say to you, we live in a world of high quality television. We live in a world where billions of dollars are being spent to produce programming that will distract and dissuade people from believing in the Gospel message of Jesus Christ. We live in the world of HDTV! So, if you think your program does not have to look good, then you are kidding yourself. You can have the greatest message there is but if no one is listening then that message has absolutely no value.

Please don't think I am being critical of ministry television. I want you to know my heart's desire is to see Christian programs become more popular and watched more than anything else on television. I do not want it to *just exist* I want it to impact the lives of the people watching. But to get there, the quality has to be equal to, if not greater than, the quality of the programs produced in the secular arena.

Most Overlooked Aspect of Television Ministry

I will not go into a lot of detail here with regards to **lighting**, but in the world of ministry, lighting is one of the most overlooked aspects I see. I have seen a lot of ministries add lighting for television and try to do it right, but with little or no direction. What they end up with is an image on television that is washed out, or the subject of the shot looks as though they are part of the background.

In order to light a stage properly, in a simplified

explanation, you will have lights **in front of, to the side of** and **behind** the subject. Most ministries add lights only to the front of the subject with no thought of adding fill lights or back lights. Often times in churches, the stage will be lit and nowhere else, so when someone is teaching and walks away from the podium they become dark.

Let me give you an example of the importance of lighting. Using a digital camera, go outside in the daylight and take a picture of something. After it gets dark, go outside and take a couple of pictures of the same object. Take the first one with a flash, and then take one without the flash. Finally, take a look at each picture and see which one has more detail. Look for detail in the object, along with detail of the object's surroundings. You will notice the picture taken in the dark with no flash has little detail and is very grainy. That is what it would be like to take and start a television program using little to no lights designed for television production. The picture taken in the dark with a flash has more detail, but often times the bright flash washes it out and there is little to no detail of the object's surroundings. The object just seems to *be there* with nothing great about it. The picture taken in the daylight will tend to look the best. Because of the the abundance of light, both the main subject and the background will have detail and clarity (depending on your camera settings).

Most television ministries fall into this category similar to taking a photo in the dark with a limited flash. They concentrate only on lighting the subject from the front and forget about the surroundings. They end up with hot spots and dark spots or a washed out look that has nothing great to offer the viewer.

A select group of ministries would fall into the final category. Those ministries are the ones with programs on television that can stand up against anything else on television and look just as good if not better. There is attention given to the subject and the surrounding aspects that make for a **dynamic picture.**

Lighting Director

A lighting director is important to having a good-looking program and is essential when you begin to decide how to light a set or stage. When you look for a lighting director, you should look for two things: experience and a stylistic vision. When I say, "stylistic vision", I mean someone who can take what you visualize and make it a reality; but more than that they can enhance the lighting in a way you might have never imagined. It is the lighting director that really makes the set or stage come to life and can make a set either look really good or if you are not careful can make a beautiful set look absolutely unusable for television.

Typically, a **lighting director** helps to plan various aspects of lighting, but also other parts of a production. Often times, they will decide on the equipment and crew, and based on the working relationship they need to have with the director and producer, they will oversee other lighting personnel and may even recommend camera positioning and angles which will help the production. Sometimes, you will find a lighting director who will also perform the function of camera operator, often referred to as a **lighting camera operator**. Whatever the case, you will need to look for someone who is not only technical, but also creative. If you remember, earlier in this book I discussed the fact television is one area of ministry that will require **technical ability** as well as **creativity**.

Cost

It would be hard to pinpoint the exact cost lighting requires because each situation calls for a different solution. The thing I want to stress here is, *lighting is not cheap*, so in developing your television ministry and initial budget expectations, make sure to **include quotes for lighting**.

When I started in television, the ministry I worked for had invested over $50,000.00 in lighting. With that investment, the program they produced looked as good as anything you would see from any other ministry on television. Depending on what your goals are, it could be more or less than that amount. So, again I would say *to get some consultation when it comes to lighting.*

Also, something to consider is what other things lighting might affect. It would be prudent to talk to an electrician and an air-conditioning technician to determine the potential need for upgrades in these areas. Understand, the cost of upgrading the electrical and air-conditioning service in your facilities could be substantial.

Creative Tool

I could go into great detail about lighting and how to light an area, but there are great books on the topic available that would be much more beneficial to you and your ministry. There is one thing I will discuss and it is meant to give you a brief overview of lighting and the ability you have with it to be creative.

Basically, when you look at lighting you must realize there is *hard light* and *soft light* and variations can be created between the two.

With hard light you have harsh shadows but a brighter light that can be used to light larger areas. This would be somewhat equivalent to a bright sunny day. With soft light you have fewer shadows and more of a natural look, but often times you cannot light large areas with soft lights. This would be somewhat equivalent to a cloudy day. Most often, you will light an area with both hard and soft light. This will give your program a more dynamic look and would be somewhat equivalent to a partly cloudy day. Again, the gradient between hard and soft can be adjusted. Think of it in terms of increasing or decreasing clouds in the sky.

Whatever the case, lighting gives you a creative tool you can utilize to make your program even more dynamic. It will bring a set or stage to life if it is done right. If you neglect having proper lighting, your overall production will suffer-- in quality and style.

Recommendations

The best thing you can do is to find someone who has experience with lighting and get his or her help from the start. It will ultimately cost you less, and in the long run your television production will look much better. You could even go so far as finding a program on television with a look you like and inquire who designed the lighting scheme. Even though a lighting director may be on full time staff for another ministry or company, they will often do work on the side as freelance consultants or even if their schedule permits, they might also become *your* lighting director.

Take Five:
Camera Operations

There are many things you need to consider when it comes to cameras and camera operators. I will discuss a few of the more important topics and try to give you an overview to help guide you in your decisions regarding cameras and camera operators. Most important, recognize the fact that the better quality picture you start with, the better end product you will have.

Camera Operators

As you have probably already guessed, a camera operator's main focus is to **operate a camera** during a production. A camera operator usually works through the direction of a director or producer. Typically, the job is not limited to just the operation of the camera. Most often, they are responsible for setting up a lot of the equipment prior to the start of a production.

Commonly, they are responsible for setting up tripods, cameras, intercom systems, monitors, and in some situations, lighting. Directors and producers will also rely on the camera operators to give creative input with regard to angles and shots to help make a more creative production.

The duties, of course, will vary based on location as well. In a church service or studio setting, a camera operator may not have duties in terms of setup and may have a little less opportunity to be creative and give creative input. Often, they will have to either follow a script or just capture the action as it happens. But, when a production is on location, there is likely to be more freedom for the camera operator to be creative with shots and position. Now, it is possible to have scripted shoots while on location, but because of the nature of field production, camera operators will often have more flexibility.

With regards to developing your television ministry, in my experience, if you want to use volunteers for a position, camera operators are the easiest to train and develop. As long as a person has a **steady hand**, an **eye for framing a shot**, and an **attention span**, they are good candidates for becoming a camera operator. Understand, it will take time for some people to pick up everything necessary to produce a good picture, and I will stress, *not everyone* is a good candidate to operate a camera. In terms of all the areas needing to be filled to produce a television program this is the one position I would say is best suited for volunteers.

Choices of Cameras

In today's world there are many options for those wanting to start a television ministry. The first decision you will need to make is what you have to spend on a camera. After you have set your budget, you need to determine the quality you are aiming to achieve, because with the multitude of cameras to choose from, the quicker you can narrow down your selections the better. Finally, you can begin searching for the perfect camera.

Cameras, like everything else, should be chosen based on what type of production you are starting and the needs you will have to accomplish your vision. Again, I want to stress **quality** and the importance for purchasing the best possible camera for your budget.

Basically, the cameras that ministries currently use fall into two categories: prosumer cameras, which are a high-end consumer or low-end professional cameras, and professional cameras.

For example, I have a few clients who annually travel overseas and do ministry. So, when I go overseas with them to document their trip I take a small prosumer HDV camera with me. Prosumer is simply a level of quality between consumer and professional. There are many reasons, but the two most important are **portability** and **safety.** Now, if I were traveling in the United States for the same client, I would choose a different field camera for the same job. The reason for that is simple: higher quality. So, determine what type of production you want to do, what quality you want to achieve and what your budget is, and go shopping.

The main advantage of a **prosumer** camera is **price**. Customarily, you get a decent picture quality for a lower price. If budget is a real concern you might look into some of the prosumer cameras. In this day and age, some of the best prosumer cameras will also shoot in HDV, which may benefit your ministry down the road. The picture quality is not as good as that from a professional camera, as you would expect. Most likely, at some point you'll have to make the decision whether or not to upgrade to better cameras as your ministry develops. As a starting point prosumer cameras might be a possible choice.

The main issue with prosumer cameras is less control, especially in a studio type environment. Typically, all **adjustment** must be done **at the camera**, and so, often times what you end up with are camera shots that look different in color and brightness. If you are not careful, the cameras may even look like they are in two different locations. I am not talking about position; I am saying completely different buildings or places.

There are more limitations you will run into and may have to work around, but that is the nature of prosumer cameras in a studio situation. You should also consider the fact, if you are using volunteers to operate your cameras, they will be the ones responsible for making adjustments and this could cause issues during a taping session.

Professional cameras will cost more and in some situations, a *lot* more. If budget is not a major concern and quality is driving your decision you will probably want to look at the professional line of cameras. Professional cameras are made for television production, so you will get the best results by using them. They give you more control and have a higher picture quality. If you are starting a studio style program or will do field production within your own country, most likely the best camera you will find would be a professional one; but, realizing *there are times* when a prosumer camera will actually be a better choice.

Support Gear

There are some other considerations when you make the choice of cameras to purchase. You will need to look at the **supporting gear** necessary to use the camera in the environment you choose.

First and foremost, if you choose to purchase **professional cameras** for a studio configuration, you will also need to purchase a **camera control unit** (CCU) for each camera. These units allow you to control the camera setup and picture from within a controlled environment. It allows a person to match the colors between the cameras and control the brightness in a multiple camera setup. This is a simplified description of what a CCU is, but this book is intended to give you a basic knowledge of television and what it takes to start a television ministry.

You will also need to purchase tripods, viewfinders, lenses and for field production -- microphones, batteries and lighting. Let me interject this about tripods, there are many different tripods on the markets but what you want to look for are **fluid head tripods**. They will give you the best results for the money you spend.

Take Six:
Audio Aspects of Television

Importance of Good Audio

When developing a television ministry, many times there is no real thought given to the audio aspects. The most common mistake churches make is either using a microphone built into a camera or feeding an audio mix from the house board into the camera or video tape recorder of some type with the expectation of good sound quality. When you are mixing audio for the house or auditorium there are many things that can and will hide the imperfections in the sound. When you listen to the audio on a television, or in a studio, you hear the imperfections. Often times, much of the audio detail is lost.

There is a wide array of tools and equipment that will help you create a good sound for your television program, but having good equipment does not mean you will have *good sound by default*. Therefore, it is important to have the **right person** to choose what equipment you actually need, along with the **right person** to operate that equipment. With the many choices of microphones, sound mixers, terminal gear and sound editing software, it is critical to get quality consultation regarding the sound.

Audio Technician/Engineer

The best way to ensure good sound is to have an audio technician or audio engineer to help you. If at all possible, my recommendation is to hire at least an audio engineer to help design and setup your initial sound for the television ministry. Then, hire him to teach the audio technicians about how to properly operate the equipment and to create good sound.

Not everyone is a perfect fit for this job. Just think about it; would you have someone who is tone deaf lead a praise and worship team? No, of course, you would not. So, when it comes to deciding on an audio technician make sure that they have the ability to hear bad sound and *understand* why it is bad. That person can always learn how to operate the equipment and make things sound better, but if they cannot hear what is wrong there is no way they will be able to correct it.

Take Seven: Control Room

A control room is basically where all the technical aspects come together. It is the **heart** of a television production and will become the **heart** of your television ministry. The **producer, director** and **technical director work** in the control room. In smaller production facilities you may also find the **audio technician** and a person who shades the cameras. The equipment necessary for the production is also located in the control room.

Basic Equipment Overview

I want to give you an idea of the equipment contained in the control room, but please remember, each ministry is different so this would not be the place to go into detail about the equipment needs.

I will discuss the basics here and I would recommend that you find a good **broadcast engineer** to give you an idea of the exact needs for you and the television ministry you are starting.

1. You will need multiple monitors. If you are not familiar with television and television equipment, a monitor is basically a high quality television set. Most of the time the first thing people notice when touring a television facility is the monitors, but they are necessary. These days, there are multiple solutions for monitors in a control room, from individual monitors to a large monitor wall that can be custom configured. **Simply said, the director should be able to see every source that may be used during the production.** If you have three cameras, you will need at least three camera monitors in the control room. If you have graphics that are added during the recording phase of production, you will need a monitor for the graphics. Additionally, you will need monitors for your preview and program outputs of your switcher. This will allow the director to see what is on air and what will soon be on air.

2. You will also need a production switcher. A production switcher can be quite intimidating for someone who has never used one, but once you understand a switcher and how it works you will have no trouble working with it. A simple analogy of the switcher's function would be comparing it to a television remote control. When a person uses a remote control to change the channel on the television set, in essence, that person is choosing what is being broadcast in his home. Of course, the consumer is choosing between television stations and networks, while a director or technical director is using a switcher

to choose what camera is being recorded, along with anything else, such as graphics, or pre-produced videos.

3. Depending on how you choose to produce your program, you may need some type of **character generator**. A character generator is a machine/ computer that creates graphics and text which will appear on the screen. The graphics may be simple text to more complex and even animated type graphics. If you choose not to do a live-to-tape program, you will probably not need a character generator because most, if not all, the graphics and text will be added in the editing process.

4. You will also need to have an audio mixer. This may be in the same room, or in a different room feeding audio to the control room and your decks. It is very important to have a separate audio mix for your television ministry from that which is in the sanctuary because of the **difference in sound needs**. Plus, you want the director and producer to have total control on what you are recording for your television ministry to create the program.

5. You will also need to have some quality **tape decks** to record your program. I have heard of ministries recording to DVD and then capturing the video from the DVD to edit. A DVD may look good at home but

the files on a DVD are very compressed and you lose quite a bit of quality if you choose to do this. **I would completely recommend against broadcasting from DVD**. Again, the quality you end up with is lacking and you have no quality control ability with a DVD once it is burned. So, as a ministry, I would recommend looking into DVCam or DVCPro formats if price is an issue. But, you may want to check into a digital beta or Beta Sp format if cost is not a major issue. You might also look into the possibility of using a HDV format if you are shooting with cameras that have that ability.

6. There is a lot more equipment that you will need to have, from camera control units to intercom systems for communication between members of the crew, so it is important that you make sure to find a consultant or broadcast engineer to help you make the decisions on what equipment will be necessary for you to begin your television ministry. **Be careful and wise when choosing your consultants, and always evaluate other work they have done along with getting recommendations. Also, it is important to get a number of quotes for equipment and installation. A better price may not mean a better deal.**

Producer

Producers, in general, play a major role in the television, film and video production. Most often, the concept for the program comes from a producer, who then oversees the entire production. Also, the producer may work on marketing and distributing the program.

In the Christian arena, often times the producer is only responsible for the look and overall decision of content in a program, because a minister or ministry board conceptualizes the program and either markets and distributes the program or hires an outside agency to do so. While in secular production, they have the responsibility to get the money to fund the program and are responsible for keeping a production within budget; in ministry production this is often not the case. Typically, the funding comes directly from the ministry or the ministry is directly responsible for finding the funds.

Now, you must realize, the Christian world of broadcasting often works a bit backwards from the secular domain. Rather than stations bidding on and purchasing programs from production companies or distributors, the ministry or producer must purchase airtime for the program. This leads to some of the differences in a producer's job description and to the use of purchasing agencies. A purchasing agent is basically responsible for finding and purchasing airtime on stations and networks for the program. It is not required that a ministry use a purchasing agent, but ministries often do.

No matter what direction you take in the role of a producer for your program, producers always will work closely with directors and the other production staff during a production. In the world of television ministry, a producer often needs to have the ability to fill other roles and they will often be required to have directing skills themselves. But, with creative ideas coming from a variety of sources the **producer has the ultimate say** on the final production.

Simply stated, producers are responsible for facilitating the program from start to finish. They are involved in every stage of the production and oversee it both in a studio and on location. Essentially, the producer is the quarterback of the production team. They give direction and make decisions to accomplish a specific game plan and to facilitate a specific end result.

Director

The director's main responsibility is to direct the overall flow of the production. They are responsible for deciding which camera shot should be recorded and when it is appropriate to use it. They will also determine what type of shot to use and the framing of a particular camera shot. They work with the producer, or even follow a script which helps guide them as to when graphics need to be added or when to roll a videotape that has been pre-produced. A director must have the ability to make quick decisions but maybe even more important, a director should be able to communicate directions to the crew just as quickly.

It is important how a director interacts with the crew and how directions are given. This is especially true with inexperienced or volunteer crew workers. As a director, a person must understand how to deal with people effectively and appropriately. When giving directions to members of the crew, even the way you word your directions are important. **Finally, you must be consistent in your directing terminology and style.**

I remember working with one director at a television station who had no experience other than what she had learned in college and had done there at the station. Sometimes, when she would give directions, the commands were so complicated it was hard to understand what she expected from the camera operator. This made the camera operators concentrate too much about what she wanted before they could perform the action. This led to a production that would lag behind the action. It is very important that camera operators be able to **act quickly** during a production-- almost without thinking. Not only was it difficult to understand her directions, she would often ask for the same move in multiple ways, rather than maintaining a consistency in her directing technique.

Remember the importance of consistency and clear concise directions. For example, a director might say, "Tilt up and pan to your left after I get off of your camera, one." With this direction every camera operator must listen and wait to see who is being asked to change the shot. So, by the time the operators figure out who is being asked to do something, they could have forgotten what needs to happen. Therefore, as a director you might want to say the following, "**Camera one**, when you're off, tilt up and pan left." This helps everyone to quickly understand what camera is going to change, when the change is going to take place and what the change requires.

The Director is responsible for the crew and their work. As a director, a person has the responsibility to approve lighting, sets, audio, camera angles and other technical aspects of the production. And, it is the director that gives direction to the crew during the taping process of a production. A director is essentially the buffer between the producer and crew, communicating issues and concerns from the crew with the producer, while communicating creative design and production concerns the producer may have *for* the crew. In many ministries, the director will also fulfill the position of producer. Therefore, all the responsibilities of both positions would fall on one person.

Technical Director

In larger and more complex productions, there can be a technical director (TD). The technical director takes cues from the director and actually pushes the buttons on the switcher. A technical director allows the director to concentrate on the other aspects of the production. This gives the director the ability to maintain the look of the program along with maintaining high standards of quality. So, the TD is basically the hands for the creative eye of a director who is creating the vision of a producer on tape.

Shading and Engineering

With professional cameras you will need a person who can **shade**. By shading, I mean a person who can maintain a consistency between the camera's color and brightness. This takes a good eye and a complete understanding of the cameras and how the camera control units work.

Let me say here, this is an area where consumer and many prosumer cameras are lacking in their ability to produce a quality broadcast. Typically, lower end cameras have little to no control aside from those on the camera. That means each camera may have a completely different look in color and brightness for your end product. You must understand, cameras are electronic, and even if they are the same model and have been manufactured at the same time and place, there is no guarantee they will have a consistent look and consistent quality.

Live-to-Tape

I wanted to address a type of taping or a taping process, for lack of a better description, and I thought here would be the best place. In the next chapter I discuss editing, but this type of program requires little to no editing. Well, let me say, the *final program* does not. Often times there are elements in the production that have required editing and then those production elements are used in creating the end production or final production.

When you hear someone say, "live-to-tape," it means exactly what it says. This is a process in which all the elements are needed for a particular production and the entire final program is recorded to tape with the director and producer **coordinating it live**. Basically, it is the same thing as a live broadcast, but rather than being broadcast at the time of recording, it is recorded directly to tape and then not altered before broadcasting. Most often, with this type of taping, there is a script being followed. While the director makes sure all the elements are used at the proper time, the producer is constantly calculating time to make sure all the elements will fit in the time allotted for the program. During this type of production, the producer basically operates as a live editor, cutting elements on the fly and communicating changes to the director allowing the director to make the appropriate changes in taping.

Take Eight:
Editing

Often, in non-broadcasting or non-professional productions, the use of the term **editing** refers to the entire post-production. Editing is a major part of the post-production aspect of television but it is not the entire process of post-production. Editing video is basically the process in which you add, remove and rearrange clips of video and audio. During this process, you may also enhance the video with various tools, filter and transitions.

Art Form of Editing

Editing is a somewhat highly technical job, but there is an **art** about it. Most often, when you edit video, and especially for ministry purposes, the objective is to have the broadcast convey some kind of story in a dynamic way. It is important to have someone who understands the technology, but also who understands the **heart of the message** the producer wants the video to carry. That person also needs to know how to use the technology to make the producer's vision become a reality. Anyone can learn how to cut and paste video and audio, but *not* everyone can make it become dynamic on the screen. It is similar to writing.

Just about anyone who has finished grade school can sit down and write something but that does not make them an acclaimed author. It takes a person with skill to make words and phrases bring the pages of a book to life. It is the same thing with editing.

Editors

I often see ministries who will tape their program and hand it to an editor who also fills the role of producer, expecting them to just put something together and get it on air. For this approach to be effective, this especially requires that you have someone who knows the **heart of the ministry** and someone who can understand how to communicate the same message on video; particularly when it comes to sermons.

You see, if a minister teaches for fifty minutes or so, and the program length is a little less than thirty minutes, you are dependant on another person to cut out a large portion of the message. That is why, if you do not have a producer making those decisions, the right editor is so important. I always tell ministers that they are the best editors of their sermons. So if at all possible, I recommend that you time the message for your program and if you run out of time close out the message for the program and then continue on for the congregation.

Non-linear versus Linear

Currently, most editing is done **non-linear**. Non-linear refers to computer based editing. Non-linear editing has become the editing form of choice with the increased processing speeds of computers and the lower prices for both computers and software. Understand, this may make the work a bit easier and faster in some respects, but it does not mean the end product is finished faster or is of better quality by default. As I have mentioned, the **quality starts at the beginning,** not the ending of your production. If you have bad quality to start with, the end product will not be better, it will be worse. So, it is very important to make sure you start out with as high of quality as possible.

One of the main advantages of **non-linear** editing is the **speed**. Because of the nondestructive, instant access style, it makes it possible to edit a video piece more quickly and more efficiently. The downside is, you will often find advanced capabilities with non-linear editing with more options for "dressing up" a production, and the initial temptation, especially for a new or inexperienced editor, is to try out every effect and transition possible. By doing this, you often do two things. First, you add more time to the editing process, therefore losing the speed advantage you have gained. Second, it often makes a program look as though the content was not very good and was in need of "dressing up" and often people will discount the quality of the message based on the packaging of the program. So, think about keeping things simple and using effects and special transitions only when necessary.

Before computer speeds increased so much in the nineties, the main type of editing used was linear editing. Linear editing is simply a process of recording from one tape to another, similar to duplicating something but a bit more complex. In this era of non-linear editing, I often hear about how linear editing is obsolete and out dated, but let me say there are still a few advantages to linear editing and an editor who understands it. First of all, linear editing is much less expensive and you have fewer conflicts with hardware, tape formats and other things. Plus, if you are doing a simple piece with cuts between each shot, it may be more efficient to edit on a linear edit system and not have to spend time capturing video. And, as an editor, it could be a great benefit to learn linear editing because you will gain more understanding of time code, basic editing concepts and more. It will ultimately make you a better editor.

Continuity

One thing I have noticed in many churches is the lack of an overall **identity.** When I speak of identity, I am simply saying churches need to present themselves in a consistent manner to the public. Corporations and companies have done this for years in their advertising, printing, office documents and now through the world-wide-web. For example, when you see something with the Nike® "swoosh" on it, automatically you recognize it is something from Nike® even without seeing the name. Why is that? It is because for years Nike® has continued to be consistent in their marketing and identity building.

You might be wondering what this has to do with editing a ministry program and a television ministry. Well, there are two reasons why I am addressing this here. One, during the editing process you have the greatest opportunity to maintain a particular look and feel in your programs. Whether you are creating a television program that will broadcast around the world or simply creating a video to be played during a church service, it is important to maintain a consistent look by using the same style, graphics, fonts and sound. You can see this in practice by just turning on your television set and watching any of the major networks.

The second reason I wanted to address this is

because for some reason in the Christian world of media and television people think we need to constantly change things. An organization may have a broadcast opening that looks good and sounds good while maintaining a consistent feel for the viewer, and then the producer or leader thinks it needs to be changed all the time to "keep people interested." Let me tell you, if you think it takes a broadcast open to keep people interested, you might evaluate whether you should even do a program.

Footage

I wanted to cover some footage that you may find important for use during the editing process. When you start your television ministry you might want to look at the possibility of shooting some special footage to be used in your programs, this footage is known as **B-Roll.**

B-Roll footage is generic footage you shoot to help you in the creation of programs. The contents of B-Roll will vary depending on what you are shooting and the type of program you decide to create. I used to produce a program for a prison ministry that included both interviews of inmates and messages recorded during special prison services. For that program, we would often request the opportunity to walk around the prison unit and shoot clips of the prison. These shots would include things like prison bars, fences, and other general prison shots. This type of footage would be classified as B-Roll, footage that may be used to fill in holes but that is not necessarily part of your main focus or script.

Take Nine: Maintaining The Television Ministry

Just like any other ministry, there are some important things that will need to be evaluated and maintained periodically.

Personnel

When it comes to your personnel, always evaluate if you are getting what you want and if the television ministry is representing the overall ministry in the way you would like. If not, you might want to think about making changes. Do not be afraid to make changes whenever they are necessary. It seems to me, every time I was in a position and it was time for me to make a change I knew it. Often times, in an effort to be kind ministries will not make necessary changes in personnel. But, you should know, if you feel the need to dismiss someone from a position, that person probably already knows your plan.

On the flip side, if you find the personnel is doing what you want and the ministry is advancing, make sure to let them know. And, when I say let them know, I mean monetarily. See, in ministry, I do believe the personnel are often neglected because of the volunteer mentality. Ministries seem to think employees should be paid less and be willing to do more than if that same employee was working in the world. But, God is a loving God and I find in the Bible where He rewards those who serve Him. Should it not also be that way in the church and for those employees who serve the ministry well?

Training

Be willing to send your staff to training seminars and classes that are available in the area. Let me make the point to be careful though and make sure it is something that will benefit them and the ministry. For example, I know how to turn on my computer and open the programs I need. I have become somewhat proficient in a number of programs and functions on my computer, while there are other programs I never use. So, for me, it would not be necessary to attend a basic computer seminar teaching someone how to turn on a computer and how to send e-mails. But, a seminar on how to use a new 3D animation software package might be one that could help me do more in my field of work.

When I was first starting out in television, working at a

church in Arlington, Texas, I was sent out to California for training in editing. The ministry there also hired freelance personnel to come in and work with me and train me in areas where I needed growth. But, after a short period of time, I was training volunteers and leading the production team. Needless to say, the amount of money I was being paid was nowhere near what the ministry had been paying for freelance personnel to create their programs prior to me taking over the department. So, the money they invested in training for me ultimately became a monetary advantage to them, along with having someone on staff to verify and make sure the same message was being sent out via television that was being taught in the church. Plus, there was someone on the staff to provide the training for others.

Many times ministries are reluctant to send employees to training. I do not have any idea why that is, but doing so it is to the ministry's benefit. Also, with the differences in television from other ministries, I would encourage you to allow your television personnel to work on other shoots on their own time. I have worked with ministries that limit their employees and do not allow them to do any work outside of what they do for the ministry. But, I have found that my knowledge and abilities have only increased with the ability to work with others. I know if I had more opportunities to work with multiple ministries early in my career, it would have only enhanced what I had to offer to all of them. If you are in television and have the chance, I would encourage you to seek out opportunities to work in different environments and ministries.

Equipment

Probably the second most overlooked item in television ministry, next to lighting, would be that of **equipment maintenance**. This is very important!

If you allowed your car to go without changing the oil, over time the engine would wear down and eventually the motor would fail. If that happened it would do two things. First, it would render the car useless without repairs, and second, it would be much more costly to repair the car at that point than it would have been to change the oil at regular intervals. This is also true about the equipment used for television -- and really, *any* electronic equipment.

I recommend one of two things. When purchasing the equipment find out what type of maintenance plans are available and take advantage of them. Or, find a good television or broadcast engineer in your area and have the engineer come in to perform regular maintenance on all your equipment. This will not only help to extend the life of your equipment, but it will also insure the program quality stays at a consistent level.

Airtime and Broadcasting

It is important that you understand and keep a watchful eye on your airtime and the stations or networks on which you are broadcasting. If you are not careful, you will be spending more money than you really want on airtime for a program or time slot that is just simply unfruitful. In Matthew 7:19 the Word says, **"Every tree that does not bear good fruit is cut down and thrown into the fire."** (NIV)

In the same respect, if you are broadcasting on a channel or network that seems to be unfruitful, you might want to reconsider whether it is wise to continue airing on that channel or network. Sometimes it may be as simple as changing the time at which you broadcast, but it may actually take dropping a station or network.

A good airtime broker, or someone who understands television and ratings, could be of great value to your ministry in this area. If you decide to pursue purchasing your own airtime, just know it can be very costly depending on the time slot you are after and the channel or network on which you decide to broadcast.

Take Ten:
Consultants, Freelance and More

Consultants

With regard to consultants, I just want to reiterate: BE CAREFUL. Make sure the person who is giving you counsel is qualified to do so. Sometimes it is hard to know if a person is qualified. Just yesterday as I began to prepare for writing some more, I received a call from a ministry asking me to come and evaluate what they were doing because the picture quality of their broadcast was not good. I asked them a few questions and came to realize, they were using broadband cameras to record their service. "Broadband cameras" are designed for broadcasting on the web not for television broadcasting. The quality is simply not acceptable for television broadcasting.

The saddest part of this whole situation started with a person who attended the church and worked for a local security company and was the one who told them the cameras would be usable. **Always get recommendations,** and if possible, look at some other work they have done. Some people may take offense at this next statement, but you must be careful when dealing with so-called "Christian brothers" because I have often seen these people prey on ministries based on their professed Christianity or a perceived mutual interest.

Freelance

When hiring freelance you will often pay a little more for their labor over someone in-house or someone with little experience. The payoff is, in most cases, you will get a better quality of work with freelancers.

There are a few things you need to consider with freelance talent and crewmembers. At times, especially with on air talent or voice talent, you will run into the issue of a limited use period. You might pay them to do some work and you will be restricted on either how long you may use the recording or how many times it can be broadcast. At the end of that usage, you will have to pay the talent **a fee** to continue using the recording. With crewmembers, such as camera operators, this is most often not the case.

License

When you use any music, video, text or still images that you have not produced yourself, those items are **copyrighted.** Therefore, you must either get permission from the person who holds the copyright or pay for a license to use the material. This varies in every situation. To protect yourself, whatever you use, make sure to have some form of **permission of use in writing**. If it is in writing you will be more protected against any type of legal proceedings.

The Internet

The question I seem to get the most is about video on the Internet. Television and the Internet are becoming more closely related each day. It is almost impossible to work in television and not know something about the Internet.

There are currently two main ways to deliver video over the Internet: **downloading** and **streaming**. [The most asked question is about **streaming video**].

Downloading means that an entire file is copied from the Internet to your computer and it is impossible for you to view the video until it has completely downloaded. If the file is not that large this method might be fine, but with larger files it is often very inconvenient. The advantage you have with this type of distribution is the speed at which you can access various parts of the file once it has been downloaded.

This type of distribution requires that the file be placed or embedded within a page on a website. You can typically do this on just about any web server.

Streaming video, on the other hand, allows a person to view the video while it is downloading. Basically, a constant stream of information is being sent to the computer and as it arrives a person can view it. This allows for greater flexibility and for live events to be broadcast over the Internet. The main disadvantage is it requires a specific server which makes the cost quite a bit more than a normal web server.

There is a third, kind of a hybrid method for streaming video, known as **progressive downloading**. With this method the file is downloaded to the computer, but a person can begin viewing the video after a portion of it has been downloaded. This simulates a streaming file but is *not real* streaming video and it does not allow you to do live events. Often, you can find servers that will help speed the download times of this type of file, but it too can be put on a variety of servers.

There are multiple file formats for you to use when you create video for the Internet. The decision as to what type of streaming and what format you use will be based on multiple factors. Whether or not you want to do live events, you want to consider cost, what type of editing system you choose to use, and how long your production will be. After you answer those questions it will pretty well lead you to the type of server you need, type of files to create and how to distribute your video on the Internet.

Field Production

I have not talked much about field production, also referred to as on location shooting, even though it is often an important part of production. There are some things you want to understand about shooting on location.

First of all, you need to be careful **where you shoot**. If you need or want to shoot in restricted areas, you must **always get permission** prior to shooting. Do not expect to just show up somewhere and shoot. Often times it takes days, and even weeks, to get approval for shooting in some locations. And, there are places that just will not let you videotape. This also pertains to private property.

It is possible to shoot on public property at times without any form of permission. That means if you would like to set your camera up on a public sidewalk and shoot cars driving down the street, it is your right to do so. You also have the right, in most cases, to shoot private or public property from a public location.

A lot of times, you will run into some over zealous security officer or someone who does not understand the laws regarding your right to be on public property, but you need to understand in most cases, as a taxpayer, you have the right to be on public property and, if you so choose, **to carry a camera** with you. I would recommend avoiding confrontations as much as possible, but make sure you get what you need when you are out on location.

Be careful shooting *people* as well. With the right to privacy laws and other things you have to consider, it is often easier to just avoid shooting a person's face. This is especially true if you are dealing with a touchy subject in your production. For example, you will often see news stories about obesity and all the people they show from the neck down. That is simply to avoid singling out that person as being the one with the problem. So, just be careful.

Finally, try to avoid recording logos, signs or anything that is trademarked and identifies a particular company. While it may be legal to show them on television in a scene of a program it may not be what you really desire. If it is unavoidable, be very careful not to make it seem as though the company sporting the sign or logo is endorsing you or your production.

[I would recommend finding a good book on communication law to help guide you while shooting on location. It will also be beneficial in other areas as well].

Take Eleven:
Closing Thoughts

Benefits

There is a wide variety of reasons why a
church television production or media ministry would
begin. Here are a few ideas to help you see how other
ministries have benefitted.

1. It almost goes without saying that **exposure for the
ministry** is one of the greatest benefits you will
receive from your television program; that is if you are
broadcasting on a station or network. It is wise to
remember it's somewhat like sending out invitations to
a party; just because they are sent does not mean
people are automatically going to show up. You need
to be careful not to expect overwhelming growth just
because of a television program.

2. You will have the ability to support other
ministries with video products. For example, you may
want to tape a puppet program for your children's
ministry or create some special greeting videos for
visitors.

3. As your capabilities increase you may want to use your production crew to create television commercials to advertise your ministry or even to send out into the community to raise support for things you are doing.

Those are just a few of the benefits you gain with having a television ministry, but believe me, as time progresses you will find a multitude of ways to use your production capabilities. There are a number of other benefits.

Purpose

No matter what you decide about organization, equipment or personnel, you need to understand the purpose of television ministry. Always maintain a biblical perspective as you develop and grow. Realize the main focus and ultimate purpose of the television ministry should be to share the Gospel. In Mark 16:15 the Word tells us, **"And he said unto them, Go ye into all the world, and preach the gospel to every creature." (KJV)** This Scripture not only reminds us of the purpose for television ministry -- but ministry in general. It is God's will that everyone hears about Christ and so *that* should always be our focus in ministry.

Final Thought

Finally, I need to mention something of great importance. Never forget that we serve the most creative being there is: **our God.** Please be careful not to fall into the trap of imitating secular productions. So many times I find churches and ministries who try to copy what they see in the world's movies or videos. My hope is that you will use the talent God has given you to produce original and imaginative videos and media and that you would maintain a high standard as you create products at the highest quality possible.

www.ingramcontent.com/pod-product-compliance
Lightning Source LLC
Chambersburg PA
CBHW031326040426
42443CB00005B/229